Follow the Horse's Lead

Finding Balance in Today's World

Rebecca J. Speelman, Ed.D.

Follow the Horse's Lead: Finding Balance in Today's World.

Rebecca J. Speelman LLC

ISBN: 978-1-7345703-3-5

www.whybalancematters.com

www.rebeccajspeelman.com

Proudly Printed in USA

DEDICATION

This book is dedicated to one of my greatest teachers, the horse! Horses have always been honest, fair, and forgiving to me. This book is inspired by a group of horses that have galloped through the pages of my life. Each one has shared their own unique life story and personality, giving me the opportunity to view the world from another perspective. I dedicate this book to all of them, especially my dear mare, April! No matter what mistakes I may make in life, she still looks at me with kind eyes and offers a warm muzzle of acceptance. It does not matter if you ride every day or are an out-of-the-saddle enthusiast, we all can benefit from what horses can teach us.

I want to thank my husband for being so supportive of my many dreams, my love for horses, and my unending passion for learning. We have been together on this wild ride called life for over 25 years. Our two children learned so much from our journey with horses, and we worked together as a team to make it all happen. I am truly blessed!

Contents

Preface

"Things happen for a reason." I am not sure this saying is easy for anyone to understand or accept at the time, but looking back, I believe it can be true. Two and a half years ago, my life came to a sliding stop due to my fight with Lyme disease, its co-infections and mold illness. Everything I had worked so hard to accomplish in my professional career became irrelevant. The years of schooling and advanced degrees, awards, titles, and experiences no longer mattered. My beloved family did their best to protect and care for me. I learned what really matters is my faith, my wellness, and finding a new purpose. I spent many hours wondering why things happen to us (like why this was happening to me), and after much prayer, I realize I must use my experiences to impact others to seek balance in today's world.

Horses have always been part of my life. My mom had the horse crazy gene, so there was already a horse in the back pasture when I was born. We always had two or three horses. I found my favorite reading spot on the back of my mom's 16 hand Appaloosa mare as she grazed in the back yard. I was given my very own horse at the age of 12, though our time together was cut short due to her cancer. She taught me to treasure each memory I made on horseback.

My parents' small farm would be considered primitive by today's standards. They made certain that we provided for and met each of our horse's basic needs. Carrying water to the old bathtub and breaking ice were mandatory responsibilities depending on the season. Horse care happened in the daylight because there was no electricity in the barn. There was no horse trailer, no barn aisle, and no cross ties. My father hand dug our fence posts with a digging iron and a broken-handled post hole digger. My first barn light was a battery-operated, pull-string model; I was so proud of it because I bought it with my own money. I also bought my first horse, an Appendix Quarter Horse weanling filly when I was 18 years old for $275, and I paid cash. I decided I was going to train her to ride. Well, what an experience. She taught me so much about what I did not know about horses. I learned you must clearly communicate and listen to the horse, ask first, and think through things from their viewpoint to accomplish what you want.

My husband and I bought my dream stallion, a black, blanketed Appaloosa as a nine-day old foal. I carefully selected a small band of broodmares based on bloodlines, color genetics and personality, and we raised a few foals. Overall, the experience led us to make connections and build relationships with some incredible horse breeders from across North America, many being old-school ranchers. They taught me a ton about letting the horse live life as God intended...as a horse, not a pet!

Each person inspired me to seek to learn more about horses and their behavior.

As our children grew and our daughter inherited the horse crazy gene, she began riding lessons, showing locally in English, then regionally and nationally in Western events. We sold my dream stallion to a breeding home in Oklahoma and we began the "show lifestyle". This journey led me to different parts of the United States, and I gained a totally different perspective about the role horses play in our lives. I learned that you can only be so book smart. Experiencing life in its authentic raw moments matter! Even with the numerous academic degrees I earned in my life, I hold steadfast to the non-negotiable need for us to experience life first-hand, both the good and the bad.

I still truly value the experiences I gained as a child on my "want-to-be-a-horse-farm" home. You see, I learned much about appreciating the things you do have, not focusing on the things you do not have. I learned work ethic and responsibility. I learned ingenuity and perseverance from my father, gained respect for horses and learned life lessons from my mother, and understood the importance of herd dynamics and gaining trust from our horses.

I tell you my story not to highlight my humble upbringings or to make my parents feel badly, but to hopefully connect with both horse owners and non-horse owners. You see not matter if we have it all or are barely getting by, if we follow the horse's lead, trust our herd, rely on ingenuity and resilience, and respect ourselves and others, we will find <u>our way</u> in this world. We just need to be open to getting back to the basics and appreciating whatever we have in our lives.

Seek to find balance, build resilience, recognize the value of work and play, embrace life changes, make mindset choices, and foster relationships. Remember to follow the horse's lead with unbridled faith. God bless!

Introduction

Follow the Horse's Lead

What does it mean to follow the horse's lead? How can we possibly compare ourselves and our decisions to that of the horse? My goal is for you to gain a newfound respect for the horse, not only as a magnificent creature, but as an amazing teacher.

From the moment of birth, horses demonstrate resilience. From their first struggles and numerous failed attempts to stand as their four legs unfold, even newborn foals are born with the innate drive to survive, to seek nourishment from their mother, and a desire to find balance in all they do.

As foals grow into weanlings, they learn to take life in stride, finding that lead changes are necessary. They soon learn to switch leads mid-stride and without hesitation. By leading with the right or left lead, they find balance as they turn, propelling themselves in the direction they want to go next. As we change leads, we need to shift our center of balance to maintain control in our own lives.

Horses position themselves to weather the storms of life, relying on their herd to help them survive and thrive. No matter what discipline we ask them to pursue with us, they act and react with passionate intention based on experiences and forgiveness, always seeking a sense of belonging and purposeful value. We can learn much from seeing things from a horse's perspective. They seek to communicate with a desire to understand and be understood.

Are you starting to see why we can learn so much from horses...if we follow their lead? One of the amazing things about horses is that we can fall in love with them face-to-face or at-a-distance. They can be part of our day-to-day responsibilities or we may a passerby who stops to gaze upon them as we travel down a country road. No matter if horses are a reality in your life OR a dream still waiting to happen, horses impact us in profound ways. Learn how you can follow the horse's lead to find balance in today's world.

A Herd Mentality

Horses, as well as people, are not meant to be alone. The most introverted person seeks a sense of belonging and value. The moodiest mare hopes to find someone to trust and rely on. We all need one another now more than ever. Expressions and body language paint a picture that cannot be fully expressed or comprehended in a virtual space. We are losing the value of close, authentic relationships that help us build trust and stability with others. We need to focus on regaining and maintaining a herd mentality. Leaders are leading alone, disconnecting more and more from their herd community. This disconnect leads to distrust and chaos, a breakdown in our circles of influence, and our rate of survival. Predators see this and take advantage of the opportunity to sabotage a herd community.

Today, with global technologies, distance learning and work-from-home options, we are spending more time connecting remotely with others and less time face-to-face. You may or may not find this enjoyable or productive. The newfound lifestyle does not come without some major concerns. The physical isolation is causing mental health issues and safety concerns. Unfortunately, most people are oblivious to the fact that we are losing a sense of community and overall well-being. Find your herd, round them up, and build real relationships before it is too late!

A Sense of Belonging

Take a moment and reflect on your own group dynamics experience with family, friends, and colleagues. Do you feel a sense of belonging? Or do you feel a longing to belong, which is making you uneasy and stressed out? We must learn ways to foster relationships in our herd community and make it a priority to gain and maintain open channels of communication, so we can strengthen our communities and ourselves in today's world.

Just as people, horses seek to belong. It is not only a want, but a need for survival in the wild. If we watch horses, we see them working together in a herd. Each horse serves a purpose and has a role in the herd. You will notice some are dominant and lead the herd, while others are content to follow...and there are some still attempting to find their best fit in the herd. Universally, they all want to know their role in the herd. They need a sense of belonging, community, and family. Human beings seek and need the same things.

If you spend time with the horse, you will notice that we share similar emotions. We just express ourselves in different ways. Body language often speaks louder than words. While horses use their entire bodies to express themselves, we also have the power of words Yet, our actions often speak louder than any words we use.

***Hoof Beats*:** When I think of genuine and honest intentions, young horses come to my mind. When they are first introduced to other horses, they are often seen expressing themselves using a rapid open-close movement with their mouth to show submission and gain acceptance. Even young horses recognize the importance of communication and starting a conversation, even with body language. Their genuine intentions usually lead to acceptance and they find their place in the herd, even as youngsters! Let us learn to start the conversation with others now.

***Out the Gate*:** Be genuine and honest in all you say and do. Have good intentions! Recognize that your actions can speak louder than words. Find your place in a herd that supports you; a place where you can trust others.

Never Lead Alone

For those of us who are the dominant type (the ones who like to lead and plan ahead), remember this.... never lead alone. Even the most dominant individuals should seek help as a leader. In a wild horse herd, the dominant mare and stallion are the leaders, but they allow others to carry out their role within the herd. People and horses who lead carry greater responsibility. With it comes greater stress, but it is sometimes self-imposed on our part. We attempt to do it all. We forget that we have the rest of our community (herd), organization, company, family, etc. to carry out their roles. By allowing and expecting everyone to contribute, each individual gains a sense of purpose, not only for the greater good of the group, but also so the leader can be most effective and efficient. Teamwork matters; never choose to lead alone.

***Hoof Beats*:** Take time to watch a wild horse herd documentary or your own herd of horses. The dominant horse will quickly appear in the herd. Once the group dynamics have been determined, the herd accepts and respects the dominant horse as the leader and trusts the decisions that horse makes for the entire herd. The dominant horse (or in our case, human) carries a lot of power, but also has a huge amount of responsibility. Great leaders must make decisions based on what is best for the entire herd. This can often cause the leader to neglect his/her own needs at the time. Take note that in a wild horse herd, there are co-leaders; one being the stallion who sires the foals and defends his harem and the other being the dominant mare who leads the herd as a family group to grazing and safety. The dominant mare rarely grazes peacefully or sleeps lying down. She is on call 24/7/365 and still takes on the responsibility of raising her own foal. Talk about multi-tasking! She is out in front leading the herd guiding them to water, food, and shelter. The stallion is at the rear of the herd, protecting them from harm, and driving away stallions seeking to take over his leadership role. The dominant mare and stallion demonstrate the teamwork and balance it takes to successfully lead a group.

We must not forget, the mare is the eyes and ears for the group and the stallion is the protector and defender, yet they are not alone. Other members of the herd step up and make a difference by supporting the leaders and fulfilling their own responsibilities. If younger horses step out of line, they are quickly reprimanded. However, they are not demoted or fired. They are corrected and forgiven, continuing to belong to the herd. The lead mare can successfully balance her roles of mother and leader because she trusts that others will follow through and do their jobs. The stallion can carry out his role as the defender for the same reasons. They have clear communication and mutual respect...and they work together as a team.

<u>Out the Gate</u>: Do not attempt to lead alone. Round up your herd. Surround yourself with competent, loyal, and honest colleagues and friends. Let them do their jobs and support you as you lead them!

Find and Pursue Your Purpose

No matter what role we play in our herd communities, each one of us has a valuable purpose. We have duties and responsibilities. Though our duties may shift from group to group, we must serve others to fulfill our purpose. There are times you may lead and other times you might follow. You do not always need to be the front-runner, the fast walker, the smooth talker. You sometimes are needed in the middle of the pack, slow and steady, a trusty and sure-footed worker. You may even be the one who brings up the rear gaining a different perspective of the entire ride. You get to see the big picture.

I believe that great leaders step back and watch from a distance. They do not micromanage the herd; they help each person find their purpose, mentor them, and then let them pursue their work. (Think about that for a minute; they loosen up their grip, allowing some free rein for others to reach their goals.) What a cool perspective; you can watch and see that the entire community (herd) is moving along toward the end goal without the leader out in front. This demonstrates the strength of a great leader. If others can step up from the middle or even rear of the pack line and lead with confidence and poise, you have done your job!

Hoof Beats: If you are looking for the all-around best trail horse, you want one that can lead, follow, and go wherever you ask it. You want the horse that is sure-footed no matter where we direct it. The absolute best horses handle a new role and place without hesitation. They multi-task with confidence. They step forward and lead the way when others balk and seem scared. They respond to our cues without hesitation. They have endurance and they are focused on their job. They are content to hang out in the middle with other horses pushing on their back sides, no matter how impatient or ignorant those around them behave. They carry the load of extra weight and supplies with steady steps and endurance. They do not rush up or down hills. They do not get flustered or famished. They are purposeful in whatever role we ask them to do. We have a tremendous amount we can learn from the horse!

Out the Gate: No matter what role you are asked to fulfill, do it with focused intention, patience, and endurance. Be willing to adapt and adjust as you pursue your purpose as a valued member of your own herd community.

Weathering the Storms of Life

Are you a weather watcher? Are you planning your days around the upcoming forecast? No matter how much we believe we are in control of our lives, unexpected "storms" appear on our radar and cause minor disturbances to major shutdowns. It might be natural events that disrupt our plans, but often, human-induced storms are the cause of our delays, detours, and challenges as we seek to accomplish too much…too fast.

Natural and man-made storms are both caused by negative and positive charges vying for attention. As a result, an energetic release occurs in the form of lightning. The decisions we make when in a charged situation can escalate into a major thunderstorm or become a passing shower. For every action, there is a reaction. Sometimes the best thing we can do is to let the words and actions of others that are raining down on us pass by and not become emotionally charged into creating a storm!

When the thunder rolls and the lightning strikes, where do you seek cover? We can certainly find a bit more balance in how we handle the storms of life by studying how the horse handles similar situations. They are resourceful and resilient, seek to meet their basic needs, and rely on gut instincts to help weather the storms of life.

Be Resourceful and Resilient

Most of us have been raised to keep our eyes on the storm, never trusting to turn our back to it. If we keep our eyes on the storm, battle against the raging wind and rain rather than seeking shelter, do we really get any farther? Could we stop and wait for the storm to pass by? Where is your place of safe refuge? Where can you go when you recognize you cannot weather the storm alone and without some protection?

Horses are said to be a fight or flight animal. I do not totally agree with this statement, as I have witnessed horses searching for a middle or common ground, a place of peace and balance. but this does not mean they never find a middle ground. Horses are taught to move away from pressure. Using body language, horses even can move us away from them. Feeding time is a great example of how horses work to find a middle ground. How about how we ourselves behave and react to pressure, such as a storm in our lives? Some of us have been taught to stand our ground and push forward, while others quickly change directions and head out of Dodge City! Do not over-react! Find a middle ground. Choose wisely!

Hoof Beats: Have you ever seen horses standing outside without any shelter during bad weather, particularly a storm with heavy rain and wind? If so, what do you recall? They are usually seen positioning their backside towards the storm, adjusting their hindquarters and legs based on the direction of the incoming storm. If you have ever tried to fight wind or water, you quickly realize why horses face away from the storm.

My amazing mare, April is our in-house weather "app" (she is an Appaloosa). April alerts us to our upcoming weather with a good 15-minute lead time due to her body posturing and behavior. She is also our absolute BEST trail horse. No matter what we encounter, she is ready and willing to face it or alert me to danger ahead. She is also our dominant mare. It is incredible to watch her and she has been quite accurate in her weather predictions. She prefers to stay outside during most storms, positioning herself well in advance. When she chooses to run to the barn for shelter, we know that the impending weather is going to be severe! Our other horses trust her and follow her lead, even those in separate pastures head for shelter! You see, the resilient and resourceful horse will run to the closest shelter if the storm becomes too fierce. A lesson we all can learn to follow.

Choose to look away from the storm and wait for it to pass. Even though it may beat on us for a few moments, the wind will soon carry the storm away. Pick your battles wisely, let the rain roll off your back and let the storm pass. Remember, there is always sunshine after the rain.

***Out the Gate*:** Remember, be resourceful and resilient as you determine what to do when storms develop in your life. You do not have to battle every storm head on or stand completely alone in the storm. Sometimes we need to be patient and wait for the storms of life to pass. Other times we need to seek shelter and help from others.

Basic Instincts

We can strive for any goal we want in our lives, but we must have access to resources that support our basic needs. Air, water, food, shelter, and rest are necessary for survival, yet many of us do not make these needs a priority. Even at the most fundamental levels of survival, horses seem to recognize the importance of taking care of themselves and their herd community. It is a basic instinct that we all can learn to follow. It is unfortunate that many people in our society neglect their basic needs of survival. In some instances, we choose to disable our natural survival instincts by handing over everything without any effort needed by the other person, creating a sense of entitlement and encouraging a lack of work ethic. Yet in other instances, we completely ignore those who are searching to meet their fundamental needs, neglecting to provide what we have readily available to share with others.

Each challenge we face helps us to develop perseverance, gain perspective during our setbacks, and learn to appreciate the simple joys of life. These life lessons are invaluable, but we must take better care of ourselves and others to meet our goals by first making our basic needs a priority. Seek clean air and water, develop heathy eating habits, and pursue physical and mental strength building activities. Few things in this world come without struggles and setbacks, so be prepared to weather the storms of life. Do not give up or quit.

Hoof Beats: If you have been fortunate enough to witness the birth of a foal and its first few hours of life, you cannot help but recognize its basic instinct to survive. The foal continues to fight until it is able to stand and walk. Finding balance is a horse's main priority. Seeking that life sustaining mare milk is instinctual. No one needs to coax or cheer on a healthy foal to stand. Even though they inevitably fall numerous times, they do not quit until they succeed. Their natural 'will to live' is why balance matters. Basic instincts push us to accomplish great things. You must balance your needs and wants to remain healthy.

Out the Gate: Learn to persevere! Learn to seek the things you truly need rather than just the things you want in life. Fight to stand back up when you fall. If you are intentionally knocked down, do not just rise up. Make the decision to **<u>rise above</u>**; take the high road and reach your goals. Learn why balance matters!

Trust Your Gut

So many times, I talk to people who share how they should have followed their gut feelings. They knew the direction they were headed. They knew it just did not feel right. It was as if intuition told them to turn back and head the other way. Yet, they kept going straight into the storm, rather than waiting or seeking cover until the storm passed. Listen to your gut! Hindsight is 20/20. We may never truly know what might have been, but I believe in the notion that when you feel like something is not right, you should trust your gut instincts. Do not make any rash decisions. The decisions others want you to make might not be in line with your values or ideas. Do what is right, not what is easy! Maybe others lack clear insight about what could happen because their vision is clouded by their emotions. Will you follow others, or will you trust your gut?

***<u>Hoof Beats</u>*:** We all say we want the willing horse, but what about the one who is willing to race down the mountain or across the river raging out of control? We want a horse that will have a can-do attitude with confidence, one that trusts what we ask it to do; yet we also certainly do not want the raging lunatic that turns into a freight train, running out-of-control and no longer paying attention to its passenger.

I envision the scene from the movie, "The Man from Snowy River" when Jim Craig asks for his brumby horse to jump down the steep cliff to chase a herd of wild horses and recapture the prized stallion. We have much to learn from that horse; he had heart and confidence in himself, and he knew the landscape beyond what his eyes could see. The Australian Outback was his home and he trusted in himself from past experiences. Finding a horse that assesses the landscape and makes informed decisions with confidence is one that has found balance with trusting itself and its rider. Without those two things, that scene could have proven deadly for both horse and rider. Finding a person who does the same makes them quite the trustworthy trail guide!

***Out the Gate*:** Trust your gut! Do not allow unwarranted fears and lack of confidence stop you from moving forward. At the same time, do not rush into the great unknown without first surveying the landscape and listening to your own intuition. Recognize that your instincts are meant to inform your choices, protect you (and others), and ultimately balance your life.

Losing Your Footing

No matter how balanced you may be in your life with work, play, family, wellness, etc., it is important to recognize the ground beneath your feet is not always secure and the path ahead will not be without challenges. Some of us are naturally better at navigating new places and obstacles. We know people who may seem extremely comfortable in new situations; they seem to embrace the unknown. We also know others who do not like going into uncharted lands without having a plan. When the footing gives way beneath us, no matter what type of person we may be, we are all on unlevel ground. We all must collect ourselves (and thoughts), slow down and evaluate how to proceed forward.

Just as life changes to lead changes…loose footing leads to speed changes. If the footing is hot and unbearable, we may rush forward because of the pain, often not paying attention to what lies ahead because it is our only way out of a difficult situation. If the path we are on starts sinking and rocks begin slipping away, some of us stop and back up, seeking an alternate route. If there is a challenge in front of you with tough obstacles to face and valleys of despair and fears, what will you do? You can see the other side, you know it is better place and your end goal is within reach, so will you push ahead, or will you decide the risk is too great? Out-of-control panic and paralyzing fear are equally deadly. We must make sure-footed decisions based on what lies ahead and the footing where we are now standing. Your greater purpose in life awaits!

Hoof Beats: When I was in my late teen years, I went on a winter trail ride with my now husband. We were riding double on a little pinto mare. She was as wide as she was tall. (Well, maybe not quite, but bareback was the way we often rode her because few saddles could fit her.) As we were taking a winter wonderland ride through the orchards, we found ourselves standing on top of snow-covered ice on a dirt road. We could feel our mare hesitate as her feet began to slip and her legs began to quiver. She was recalculating her balance. She stood still for a moment. The area of ice was so wide, we could not dismount. We were along for the ride with no exit option. We did our best to balance ourselves as one person on her back, giving her full extension of the reins, and placing our trust in her to navigate across the ice. We easily could have gathered the reins tight and stifled her natural instincts. She could have slipped and fallen on that ice, but she took each step with precision and patience. Once she found balance, our little mare moved with confidence in her steps and regained her footing on the other side of the icy patch. I recall that experience like it was yesterday because of its impact on how we should navigate our own lives when we lose our footing in unexpected places.

Out the Gate: For every action there is a reaction. Consider the big picture and decide how to proceed. Do not freeze up and let fear take over your steps. Move forward and take each step with confidence and faith.

He gallops into the clash of arms. He mocks at fear and is not frightened; Nor does he turn back from the sword. The quiver rattles against him, The glistening spear and javelin. He devours the distance with fierceness and rage.

Job 39:21-24

Run Your Own Race

How many of you can relate to hearing someone say those four words at some point in your life? RUN. YOUR. OWN. RACE. Do not compare yourself to others. As a runner those words connected to me during my high school years. Those same words are what Penny Chenery is said to have told Secretariat, an amazing thoroughbred racehorse. He was the winner of the 1973 Triple Crown. Her story alone is remarkable, but together with Secretariat, they made a lasting impression on me. In the movie based on their lives together, Penny tells Secretariat that she ran her race and now it is time for him to run his own. The race is a metaphor for our life, our goals, and our dreams. Therefore, I tell each person who reads this book...apply it to what best fits your own life...run your own race. Do not compare yourself to anyone else. You are valuable and your life story is unique. As no two horses are ever alike, the same holds true for each one of us. We each have a special purpose in this world.

Go Your Own Way

I am sure you know two people who ended up at the same place at the same time but chose different routes to get there. It could be a trip to the grocery store, a vacation spot, or a career path. Two people could be working in the same job position, be given the same title, pay scale, and responsibilities, but their journey to that position might be totally different. One may have chosen a path of hands-on learning and performance, and the other chose a four-year college degree and academic accomplishments. Both met their goal! The key is to go your own way and pursue whatever route necessary to get where you want to go in life. Destinations have multiple access points. Be a trailblazer!

Hoof Beats: Are all thoroughbreds destined to be fast? Does each horse have the same stride length or movement? Why are some gaited and others not? If you take time to watch and study the patterns and behaviors of horses, you will notice each one has its own habits, personality traits, and talents. Size may or may not matter. Age may or may not matter. If horses need to accomplish a goal, they typically find their own way to get it done. It may not even be based on talent; it could be based on having the heart to do something!

We have a gelding who travels with a different gait, one that is especially noticeable at the walk. Cooper is not lame, but it is obvious his movement is not typical. (Our daughter says he has swag!) In many ways his movement is what uniquely identifies him. We have traveled to multiple states and horse shows, yet people will come up to us and tell us they know him. Beyond his personality and talent, his gait is what is recognizable about him. He was born with a club foot, which led to his odd movement. However, it does not stop him from being able to do his job and do it well. He is always willing, he listens to his rider, and he truly seems to believe in himself. He goes his own way with confidence and poise!

Out the Gate: Do not let anyone sell you short of reaching your goals. You may use a different method, be on a different time schedule or travel a different route to your destination goal. In the end, you can accomplish your goals. If there is a will, there is a way! Believe in yourself, even if no one else seems to believe in you. Go your own way!

Finding Your Stride

You may feel pressured to meet the expectations of others not only based on performance, but also a designated timeline that has been created without you in mind. Deadlines, benchmarks, standards are often imposed by others, but have no definitive impact on your success. Maybe you are a great basketball player, but no one gives you any attention because you are not tall. Maybe you have (had) people telling you that you should or should not pursue your dreams. No matter what others say, seek your purpose and pursue it. You can be 17 years old or 71 years old; you still have value and purpose in this world.

You do not have to live on someone else's timeline. You can go against all odds and still accomplish your goals. (Just be certain they are YOUR goals.) Just as young children are stressed out by society-imposed performance standards and timelines, the same thing happens to adults (AND HORSES). Personally, I know last names are tied to certain athletic, musical, or academic expectations in my hometown. Judging others can be difficult to avoid, but we must caution ourselves to not fall prey to prejudice. Give every person and horse a chance to prove themselves…on their own.

Some of us do not reach our peak performances until later in life. Some of us break from the starting gate ready to lead the 'race of life' from start to finish. One STRIDE does not fit all. We all travel through life at different speeds with different lengths of stride. And we saddle up for this "wild ride called life" in the same fashion. Do not let pre-conceived expectations change your stride.

***Hoof Beats*:** Have you ever met a horse that was not mentally or physically ready for the expectations placed upon it? Just think about how many young horses are sold as so-called 'rejects', when, they might just be slow growers.

We had a gelding that we brought into our herd when he was four years old. He had an amazing disposition, quirky and friendly, good bloodlines, and a great foundation under saddle. However, he lacked A LOT in the coordination department. I genuinely believe he did not know what to do with his hind feet until he was six years old. I bought him protective leg wraps, pastern protectors, sent him to a trainer and brought him back home. I took him to a training clinic and was told to sell him...to not waste my time. I could have been impatient and selfish and sold him, but I chose not to. (He reminded me that I was once that late-blooming teenager, attempting to find my stride and balance.) Once he grew into himself, finding his own balance and coordination, he became one of the smoothest riding horses we have ever owned. Few people would have waited a year and a half on a horse to see if it would mature into finding its stride. We live in an 'I want it now' world. It seems as if everyone and everything must meet benchmarks at the same time, perform at the same level, and meet the social status-quo.

***Out the Gate*:** Reflect on our own experiences. Find our own stride on this journey called life. Do not try to be someone you are not. Each of us is unique. Choose to give one another some grace and space. We can experience less stress, find greater joy, and gain a balanced perspective of what really matters in life. We might even enjoy each stride of our ride. We all need to find our own way and run our own race!

Life Changes, Lead Changes

Just imagine you are relaxing in the warm sun with your family or some friends one day and the next you are told you must immediately move to a new town for at least the next year. During that time, you learn a lot about life on your own and what is expected of someone your age. You are offered a new job and you relocate again. This time you impress your boss, and you seem to have untapped potential. You are not so confident as you only have worked at the new place for a few months. Yet, your boss feels like it is time for a promotion. You are given a new space to work…with the caveat that you must not only balance your existing responsibilities but carry the load and be responsible for someone else at the same time. You experience a learning curve. You resist a little bit, but want to please your boss, so you do your best work with all that is thrown on you. Unlike some of your colleagues, who just have not found their stride yet, you continue to do such a good job. They decide to add a completely new job title with "all other duties as assigned" to your workload and now you are the all-around business partner. You seem to be fast-tracking to the top…or so you think! Life happens….and out-of-the blue, you change directions again with such a sharp lead change that it causes things to start flying out of control. You become a so-called train wreck. Sound familiar to anyone? Well, this could be a story about your life…

Nothing in life is certain and as much as we would like things to last forever, there will inevitably be changes in our journey. Things will be gained, things will be lost, and some things will never happen as planned. We may only have one chance to make the right decision or we may be given lots of opportunities to learn from our mistakes. The only certain thing is that we need to learn how to accept change and switch leads, or we are going to be unbalanced and out-of-control when life changes occur.

***Hoof Beats*:** Let us look again at that story I just shared and see how it parallels with the horse. Just imagine you are relaxing in the warm sun with your mom and pasture mates one day and the next you are loaded into a horse trailer headed to a totally new home for at least the next year. During that time, you learn a lot about life and what is expected of someone your age as a yearling. You are bought by a new person and you relocate again. This time you impress your new owner. They feel you have a lot of potential, so they hire a trainer to help you reach your full potential. You are not so confident as you only have a few months of training completed and no one has ridden you yet. Your trainer feels like it is time for a promotion…with the caveat that you must not only balance your existing responsibilities, but also carry the required tack and be responsible for someone riding you. It is time to combine all the things you have learned even though you are not fully done growing yourself. It is a learning curve. You resist a little bit, but want to please your boss, so you do your best to accomplish all that is thrown on you, including different tack and riders. And unlike some of your other horse family and friends, who just have not found their stride yet, you do such a good job, your owner decides to add a completely new job title with "all other duties as assigned" to your workload. They think you can be that all-around performance horse. You seem to be fast-tracking to the top of the horse industry…and then life changes. You mentally have a break down, you physically cannot handle the workload, or you never spent enough time gaining the foundational skills necessary to handle all the pressures put on you. When life changes, your leads change. You lose your balance and life careens out-of-control. (Now remember, we are talking about the horse right now, not you. The resemblance to our own life story is remarkably similar.)

***Out the Gate*:** Learn how to change leads as life changes. Reposition, recollect, and focus on where YOU are headed next, not where you came from. If there are gaps in what you learned, it is not too late to gain that knowledge and fill in the gaps. Do not live with constant fear about what has already happened or what might happen. Have confidence in yourself, so that when life changes you are ready to change leads for what lies ahead.

Turn Out Time Required

How many hours do you work in a day? How many days per week? Not just at your job, but also with your family? Do you schedule any quality down time into your life? (Optimally 30 minutes minimum each day is what you need as quality down time to maintain a healthy balance of mind, body, and spirit.) I have no idea what makes you happy, but you should make time for turnout each day! Did you know the average person experience career burn out at 32 years of age? (Yes, multiple sources say the same thing.) That is way too early to retire, so what can we do. Some employers choose to offer more vacation time than others. What is the benefit? Productivity and improved health/wellness are the two biggest benefits when providing humans with greater vacation time. (It is the concept of turnout before burnout).

In addition, employers cannot seem to find enough people to hire to sustain the manual labor workforce today. These jobs require not only mental stamina, but physical strength and resolve. These employers are often willing to pay higher wages and provide greater vacation benefits because they need workers who are focused on willing to work hard, focus on being safe, and remaining healthy so they can continue working for them.

Turnout or Burnout

If you do not make time for turnout in your own life, it will lead at some point to burn out, possibly with health issues and disease. I speak from my heart and experience. My own life was not fulfilled, it was overfilled. Accolades, awards, fast-track job promotions, advanced college degrees, and all other duties assigned; I said YES to everything! My career became my laser focus. My turnout time soon became non-existent. We owned eight horses and I rode one of them maybe two times a year. I did make time to enjoy them. I worked so hard to be able to help finance our facilities and well-bred horses, but my career and caring for our children were my responsibility and passion. I barely found balance with those two things. When I was attacked by Lyme disease and its co-infections, I could not switch leads and I lost control. My body could not handle the stress. Nothing is more important than your own balanced wellness!

<u>Hoof Beats:</u> In the wild, horses take time to rest and play. Watch a wild herd of horses and you will see some sleeping in the middle of the afternoon, some peacefully grazing, and others playing and chasing one another for exercise. Domesticated horses have lost the natural ability to determine when and how to balance work and play. Oftentimes we hear about famous, high dollar horses, the ones bringing in sizeable cash earnings and year-end titles like top business executives. Yet, I am not sure they are having an increase in vacation time. These horses spend their life on the road like rock stars, yet they rarely make a comeback for encore performances later in life. They travel to temporary stalls in a new town every other week and they very rarely have turn out time in their own paddock or field for fear of injury. Just like us, they often develop bad habits that alleviate anxiety, boredom, and even pain. Often, burnout starts slowly, and they experience inconsistent performance, lameness issues, ulcers, and attitude problem before the total breakdown happens. It takes a rider/trainer/owner who pays attention to the horse, taking into consideration their workload, work schedule, and following the horse's lead. This is the only way to stop burnout from causing permanent damage. Often, the best choice (though difficult) is pulling their shoes and sending them off barefoot into the pasture, so they recharge and reconnect with what it means to be a horse.

Out the Gate: *Barefoot in the grass is where it is at!* This is one of my new favorite sayings. Find time to take off your shoes, enjoy the simple pleasures of life, and reconnect with what makes you happy. You will find a sense of rejuvenation and balance! Seek turnout, before you burnout!

Kick Up Your Heels

What are your favorite things to do when you have free time? Some people enjoy peace and quiet, while others enjoy socializing and action-filled days and nights. Each person is uniquely different when it comes to kicking up his/her heels and enjoying free time. No matter what you find to be enjoyable, the key is to enjoy yourself. Make plans ahead of time, build up excitement for what is planned, and most importantly, be certain to follow through with enjoying it. Often, we talk a lot about what we could do; we daydream about a day at the beach/lake, in the woods, on the golf course, or best of all, on the back of a horse. But then we let other things take priority over our turnout time. I am not talking about important family responsibilities or emergency situations, but we often come up with excuses or have other people dissuade us from our free time plans. Carve out the time to be free and kick up your heels!

Hoof Beats: Watch horses as they are led out to pasture, especially if they have been stalled for a few days due to their work schedule or inclement weather. They toss their heads, lift their tails, kick up their heels, and enjoy freedom! They snort, prance, spring into the air, lift their knees, and express pure joy as they are set free. Not long after the race around the paddock, they seek out that perfect spot (often filled with mud/dirt) to roll off. They are actually detoxing themselves. After giving themselves a cleansing massage, they follow up with some quiet grazing and possibly a nap. Sounds like the perfect spa day to me!! Who else wants to sign up to be led out to an open field of lush grass, soak up some sunshine, detox, and kick up your heels for the day?

<u>Out the Gate:</u> Kick up your heels and enjoy a day doing your favorite things. You will release pent-up energy, detox your entire system, and find a sense of inner calm and a clearer mind. I encourage you to take a moment right now and arrange some self-turnout time.

You Can Lead a Horse to Water…

Do you remember the rest of this saying? "You can lead a horse to water, but you cannot make it drink." It is true for horses and humans alike. Even though it is one of our basic needs, unless we thirst for it, we do not choose to drink it. Of course, water can be replaced with practically anything in this statement and it still holds value. Unless the other person or horse wants that which you are offering them, even if it is beneficial, you will not change their mindset. Attempting to control others and their choices will only lead to frustration and resentment. It does not mean we quit attempting to help them, but our approach may need to change. Think of offering a glimpse of what the change may look like, open the door for them, and then just be patient and wait. It can take quite some time, so be prepared for the long journey ahead.

Attitude and Mindset

It is a joy to find someone who is positive and pleasant, sees life with a "glass half full" mentality, and deeply appreciates everyone and everything. They are excited to see you, do things to please you, and you look forward to spending time with them. However, we often encounter someone who is negative, sees life as 'gloom and doom', and seems to appreciate no one or thing as being good. They are sullen, distrusting, and sometimes downright rude. We often attempt to avoid them because of their attitude. (You may even fit one of these descriptions right now and that is okay!)

Our attitudes and mindset about ourselves and others are shaped by the world in which we live. Each of us has a story, one with experiences that have been carved deep into our being, and what we display on the outside may only be a protective shell for what is really happening deep down inside our mind. Before you judge someone, take time to get to know them a bit. I think you might appreciate if others did the same for you. (I know a mare who just needed me to do that very thing.)

***Hoof Beats*:** We all know her; she never seems happy. The moody mare! She stares at you from the back of her stall, eyes fixed and ears pinned as soon as you enter with the halter. What makes her like this? Most of us do not even attempt to find out. We just avoid her, sometimes leaving her all alone in isolation.

Yet, we all love him; he nickers at the sound of footsteps on the barn aisle. The flamboyant and social gelding. He cannot see who is coming and honestly does not care who you are. He is just excited that someone is there. He breathes warm kisses on anyone he can reach, always gentle but persistent to gain someone's attention.

Unlike humans, horses express themselves with honest, unfettered emotion. They do not hide or attempt to cover up their feelings. They do not drink the water just to please or appease us. They do not pin their ears and attempt to bite us without a reason, a back story. They live what they learn and learn what they live. I witnessed a moody mare soften with love, kindness, and most importantly, patience. Earning her trust has been indeed special. (I like to say that she is highly selective about who she allows into her herd and heart.) We cannot change anyone's past experiences, but we can possibly change their mindset. And we can do the same for ourselves with a little practice.

Out the Gate: Recognize we all have a back story. Our attitude and mindset cannot be changed by others unless we are willing to allow others into our herd. The same holds true for others as we interact with them. We all live what we learn and learn what we live. Change is always possible!

Letting Go of the Reins

I remember being told, **no matter what**, do not let go of the reins. Today, I see this as a true test of trust and balance. Riders are often seen pulling on their reins, which in turn places an enormous amount of pressure in the horse's mouth through the bit. Depending on the type of bit, the pressure can be severe. Of course, we are to use the reins as aids in rating direction and speed, but a lot of riders use the reins as a leverage tool for an unbalanced seat. Many riding instructors attempt to help their students achieve balance in the saddle with lessons like no-stirrup November. It is a great idea that works with focused effort and practice. We must strengthen our core to become a balanced rider.

How can we take what we learn from horseback riding and apply it to our 'out-of-the-saddle' life experience? I believe we must develop a strong inner core and trust our horse (and ourselves) when seeking balance without constantly relying on the reins. We are often too tight on the reins, restricting ourselves (and our horse). We think they can compensate for our own imbalances in life. Yet, we end up restricting our God-given talents. Stop controlling and start trusting!

Hoof Beats: Watch a young horse at play in the field and you will see raw, natural talent. They often exhibit skills that totally amaze me. Based on bloodlines and body conformation, many can maneuver themselves in ways that mimic that of exceptionally trained adult horses. (We may be giving ourselves more credit than we deserve, as many horses naturally find balance in all they do.) Each one of them has God-given genetics that allow them to excel in areas or discipline without a rider's cue or reins. From sliding stops to spins, from running walks to piaffes, horses do not need human help to demonstrate their natural skills. Sometimes we even use tools to stop them from utilizing their gifts because they do not fit our plans for them. We stifle gaits in horses, we use certain bits and reins to gain a desired headset, and spurs and hobbles to control movement. We alter the natural talents of others to meet our needs. We change them so we balance ourselves and enjoy the ride. Does it sound familiar to your own life and expectations from others?

***Out the Gate*:** Give yourself a chance to find what you are good at; do not rein yourself in based on what others think you can or cannot do. Of course, we have reins to help guide us, but sometimes the best thing we can do is find our core center of balance. Work on letting go of the reins and building trust.

Unbridled Faith

There is no greater trust than that of an unbridled faith in your future. No matter what has happened, is happening now or might happen in the future, know that you have value and purpose. If you recognize how powerful following the horse's lead can be, you will develop an unbridled faith in others (and yourself). Each one of us will leave behind a story, a legacy that will impact at least one person in this world. Will you leave a legacy that exemplifies your faith?

Hoof Beats: Tears rolled down my cheeks as I watched in awe. I was about eighteen years old and attending a horse expo in Pennsylvania. The arena was dark, except for the spotlight on a beautiful horse with a rose-laced neck rope. Lynn Palm was poised and at ease as her horse loped around the arena, the spotlight glistening upon his coat as it followed their every move. The horse was Rugged Lark. I had never seen a horse ridden without a bridle and perform maneuvers with such grace, precision, and style. I spent most of that weekend replaying that horse in my mind. I wish I would have been watching Lynn Palm more closely. How trusting and faithful she was aboard Rugged Lark in that arena in front of several thousand people. Crowd noises, bright lights, different footing, and a strange location; all the distractions were there…yet their focus remained unchanged. They rode together as a team with unbridled faith. A faith that we should not only have with our horse, but more importantly, with ourselves and our Creator.

***Out the Gate*:** Do not worry about what might happen if you try and fail. Trust in yourself. Trust that there is goodness in our world. Most importantly, trust in your faith of the unknown. Fulfill your purpose; find balance by living with unbridled faith. Follow the horse's lead!

Finding Balance

As you move beyond the time spent reading this book, my hope is that you carry the following fifteen tips with you on this "wild ride" called life:

1. Be genuine and honest in all you say and do. **Have good intentions**! Recognize that your actions can speak louder than words. Find your place in a herd that supports you; a place where you can trust others.
2. **Do not attempt to lead alone. Round up your herd.** Surround yourself with competent, loyal, and honest colleagues and friends. Let them do their jobs and support you as you lead them!
3. No matter what role you are asked to fulfill, do it with focused intention, patience, and endurance. **Be willing to adapt and adjust** as you pursue your purpose as a valued member of your own herd community.
4. **Remember, be resourceful and resilient** as you determine what to do when storms develop in your life. You do not have to battle every storm head on or

stand completely alone in the storm. Sometimes we need to be patient and wait for the storms of life to pass. Other times we need to seek shelter and help from others.

5. **Learn to persevere!** Learn to seek the things you truly need rather than just the things you want in life. Fight to stand back up when you fall. If you are intentionally knocked down, do not just rise up. Make the decision to **rise above**; take the high road and reach your goals. Learn why balance matters!
6. **Trust your gut!** Do not allow unwarranted fears and lack of confidence stop you from moving forward. At the same time, do not rush into the great unknown without first surveying the landscape and listening to your own intuition. Recognize that your instincts are meant to inform your choices, protect you (and others), and ultimately balance your life.
7. **For every action there is a reaction.** Consider the big picture and decide how to proceed. Do not freeze up and let fear take over your steps. Move forward and take each step with confidence and faith.
8. **Do not let anyone sell you short of reaching your goals.** You may use a different method, be on a different time schedule or travel a different route to

your destination goal. In the end, you can accomplish your goals. If there is a will, there is a way! Believe in yourself, even if no one else seems to believe in you. Go your own way!

9. Reflect on our own experiences. **Find our own stride on this journey called life.** Do not try to be someone you are not. Each of us is unique. Choose to give one another some grace and space. We can experience less stress, find greater joy, and gain a balanced perspective of what really matters in life. We might even enjoy each stride of our ride. We all need to find our own way and run our own race!
10. Learn how to change leads as life changes. **Reposition, recollect, and focus on where YOU are headed next, <u>not</u> where you came from.** If there are gaps in what you learned, it is not too late to gain that knowledge and fill in the gaps. Do not live with constant fear about what has already happened or what might happen. Have confidence in yourself, so that when life changes you are ready to change leads for what lies ahead.
11. *Barefoot in the grass is where it is at!* This is one of my new favorite sayings. Find time to take off your shoes, enjoy the simple pleasures of life, and reconnect with

what makes you happy. You will find a sense of rejuvenation and balance! **Seek turnout, before you burnout!**

12. **Kick up your heels and enjoy a day doing your favorite things.** You will release pent-up energy, detox your entire system, and find a sense of inner calm and a clearer mind. I encourage you to take a moment right now and arrange some self-turnout time.
13. Recognize we all have a back story. Our attitude and mindset cannot be changed by others unless we are willing to allow others into our herd. The same holds true for others as we interact with them. **We all live what we learn and learn what we live.** Change is always possible!
14. Give yourself a chance to find what you are good at; do not rein yourself in based on what others think you can or cannot do. Of course, we have reins to help guide us, but sometimes the best thing we can do is find our core center of balance. **Work on letting go of the reins and building trust.**
15. Do not worry about what might happen if you try and fail. Trust in yourself. Trust that there is goodness in our world. Most importantly, trust in your faith of the

unknown. **Fulfill your purpose; find balance by living with unbridled faith.**

Follow the horse's lead!

I WOULD LOVE TO HEAR FROM YOU!

Contact me: dr.rebecca.speelman@gmail.com

I would welcome an opportunity to speak at your next event.

www.whybalancematters.com

www.rebeccajspeelman.com

Rebecca J. Speelman, LLC

Additional Resources of Interest

Follow me on Facebook:

Rebecca J. Speelman, Ed.D.

Rippling Rock Ranch – Follow the Horse's Lead

Romans 12 Living

Why Balance Matters

www.ingramcontent.com/pod-product-compliance
Lightning Source LLC
LaVergne TN
LVHW010544100826
845148LV00013B/2592

* 9 7 8 1 7 3 4 5 7 0 3 3 5 *